W9-BKI-636

NINJAS

by Carla Mooney

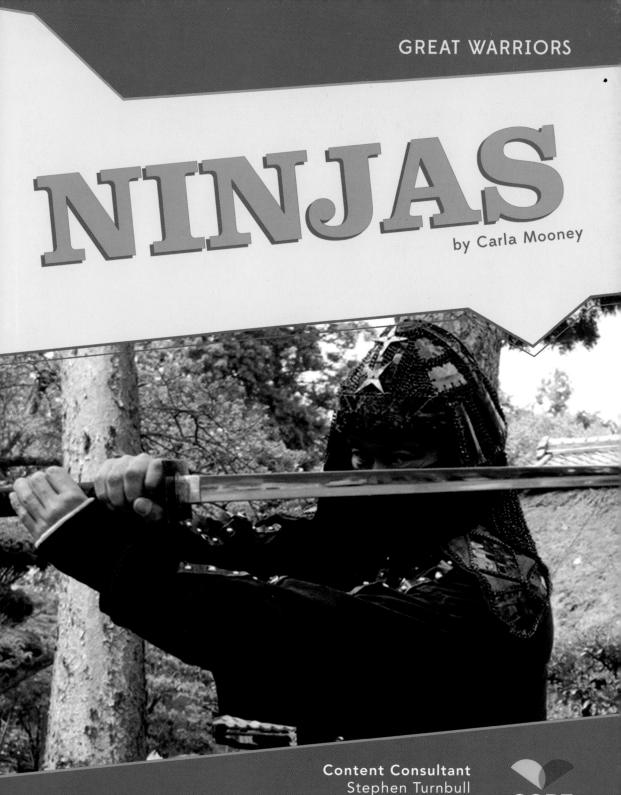

Content Consultant
Stephen Turnbull
Visiting Professor of Japanese Studies
Akita International University, Japan

CORE
LIBRARY

Published by ABDO Publishing Company, PO Box 398166, Minneapolis, MN 55439. Copyright © 2013 by Abdo Consulting Group, Inc. International copyrights reserved in all countries. No part of this book may be reproduced in any form without written permission from the publisher. The Core Library™ is a trademark and logo of ABDO Publishing Company.

Printed in the United States of America, North Mankato, Minnesota
112012
012013

♻ THIS BOOK CONTAINS AT LEAST 10% RECYCLED MATERIALS.

Editor: Lauren Coss
Series Designer: Becky Daum

Cataloging-in-Publication Data
Mooney, Carla.
 Ninjas / Carla Mooney.
   p. cm. -- (Great warriors)
Includes bibliographical references and index.
ISBN 978-1-61783-726-5
1. Ninja--Juvenile literature.   1. Title.
355.5--dc22
                                        2012946374

Photo Credits: Toshifumu Kitamura/AFP/Getty Images, cover, 1; Mike Clarke/AFP/Getty Images, 4; DeAgostini/Getty Images, 7, 13; Hemera/Thinkstock, 9, 32; Werner Forman/Universal Images Group/Getty Images, 10, 24, 34; Red Line Editorial, 15; Dorling Kindersley RF/Thinkstock, 26; Universal History Archive/Getty Images, 16; Werner Forman/Glow Images, 18, 45; Kazuhiro Nogi/AFP/Getty Images, 21; Atta Kenare/AFP/Getty Images, 23; Itsuo Inouye/AP Images, 28, 40; Demetrio Carrasco/Dorling Kindersley, 31; Shutterstock Images, 39

CONTENTS

CHAPTER ONE

SHADOW ATTACK!

A young boy crept noiselessly through a dark house. The house belonged to a monk named Homma Saburo. Rain fell violently outside. Wind whipped in the night. The boy was Hino Kumawaka. He was only 13 years old. According to legend, he was about to become the first ninja assassin.

Ninjas were ancient Japanese assassins and spies. Today people still study ninja arts, including ninja fighting techniques.

The Youngest Assassin

Hino lived in Japan in the 1330s. Hino's father had been accused of a plot against the general of the Japanese emperor's army. The general was known as the shogun. Homma ordered that Hino's father be executed as punishment. Young Hino vowed revenge against the monk for his father's death.

Hino was being held in Homma's house. Hino faked illness for several days to prepare for his attack. Each night, he snuck out from his room and gathered information about the layout of Homma's house. He waited for a dark, stormy night that would conceal

Kunoichi

Most ninjas were male. But a female ninja might have better luck in some missions. A female ninja was known as a *kunoichi*. She often played an important role in ninja operations. Few men suspected a woman of being a spy. A kunoichi could disguise herself as a servant or maid to gain access to the enemy's palace. A kunoichi could hide small weapons in her dress or in her fancy hairstyle. She could also use her fan as a weapon.

Female servants often worked closely with Japanese leaders. By pretending to be a servant, a kunoichi could get into places a male ninja could not.

him. Then Hino crept silently through the house. He stopped when he reached the room where Homma was sleeping.

A sword lay beside the sleeping man. A light burned in the room. Hino worried he would be seen in the light if Homma woke when he drew the sword.

Hino had a clever idea. It was summer. He knew many moths were flying in the garden. He quietly opened a door leading outside. The lamp's flame drew the moths inside the house. They flew into Homma's room and swarmed around the lamp. When the moths covered the lamp, the room fell into darkness.

Hino moved forward. He slowly drew Homma's sword. He held the blade's point to Homma's chest and kicked the man's pillow aside. Then Hino drove the sword into Homma's body, killing him.

After killing Homma, Hino ran away. He faced one last obstacle outside the house. It was a moat.

Ninja Legends

Ninja legends grew as ninjas became more common in the 1300s. Some people believed ninjas had superhero powers. People whispered the secret warrior could become invisible. Others told stories of ninjas who could fly over castle walls. Really, ninjas were skilled fighters who were experts at stealth and secrecy.

Many Japanese homes and castles were surrounded by moats.

He could not jump across the water because it was too wide. Hino climbed to the top of a bamboo plant growing above the water. Under his weight, the tip of the bamboo plant bent down across the moat. Hino landed safely on the other side. The first ninja assassin disappeared into the dark night.

CHAPTER TWO

HISTORY OF THE NINJAS

The ninjas were secret warriors of Japan. They were most common from the 1400s to the 1600s. They traveled throughout Japan and sold their skills to anyone who would pay them. Like Hino, ninjas used shadows and secrecy to carry out their missions. They were expert spies. They were skilled in hand-to-hand combat. Ninjas often used disguises to sneak into enemy armies. They gathered

Ninjas were experts at secrecy and spying as well as fighting.

Ninjas for the Shogun

Not all ninjas worked as mercenaries. Some could be loyal. After an attack on a group of ninjas in 1581, many ninjas settled in the Mikawa province. The local lord, Tokugawa Ieyasu, ordered that the ninjas be treated with kindness. In 1582 a rival lord wanted to kill Tokugawa while he was traveling. Because Tokugawa had helped the ninjas, they helped him return home safely. The ninjas remained at Tokugawa's side as he grew more powerful. In 1562 the ninjas raided Tokugawa's rival's castle. Tokugawa appointed ninjas as his personal bodyguards. When Tokugawa became shogun in 1603, the ninjas guarded his castle. They also fought in wars for the new shogun.

valuable information. Since their beginning, these great warriors have captured the imaginations of people around the world.

Early History

The history of the ninja is as shadowy as the stealthy warrior. Much of their work was done in secret. One of the first records of ninja-like spying occurred in the year 940. Taira Masakado led a rebellion against the Japanese emperor. Taira Yoshikane, Taira Masakado's uncle, supported the emperor. He hired an agent to

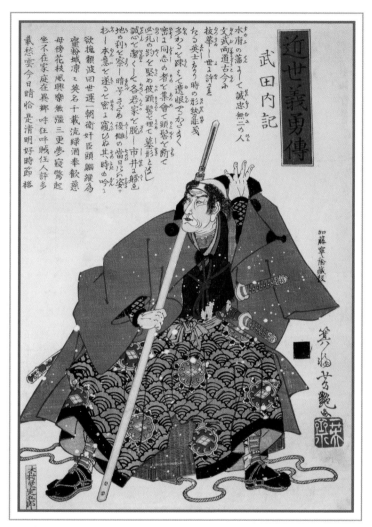

近世義勇傳

武田内記

Japanese lords often hired ninjas to do their dirty work.

spy on Taira. The spy posed as a servant. He passed information about Taira Masakado's defenses to Taira Yoshikane. This secrecy was an early example of *ninjutsu*, the set of skills used by ninja warriors.

The Anti-Samurai

Samurai were Japan's elite warriors. They often came from upper-class families. They lived, fought, and died by a strict samurai code. The samurai highly valued honor, discipline, and loyalty. They remained loyal to one lord. On the other hand, ninjas were often commoners from poor farming communities. They worked as mercenaries. They had no loyalty to one leader. They were willing to use trickery and deceit to achieve their goals. These key differences gave ninjas important roles during times of war.

Power Struggle

From the 1100s onward, ninja methods were part of Japanese warfare. Japan was divided by civil war during this time. The emperor had little power. But the emperor's shogun was a powerful military ruler. Throughout Japan, local warlords called *daimyos* fought each other. They usually paid little attention to the emperor. Sometimes they even ignored the shogun's orders. The daimyos wanted more land and power. Some hoped to overthrow the shogun and take over Japan. The daimyos hired samurai and ninjas to do their fighting.

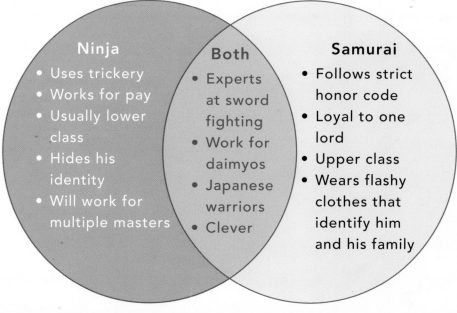

Ninja
- Uses trickery
- Works for pay
- Usually lower class
- Hides his identity
- Will work for multiple masters

Both
- Experts at sword fighting
- Work for daimyos
- Japanese warriors
- Clever

Samurai
- Follows strict honor code
- Loyal to one lord
- Upper class
- Wears flashy clothes that identify him and his family

Ninjas versus Samurai
The diagram above compares and contrasts ninjas and samurai. How were these two warriors the same? What made them different? What additional characteristics of ninjas and samurai could you add to this diagram?

Each side of the war needed deceptive spies or deadly assassins. The samurai believed working in secret was dishonorable. They would not perform these missions. Instead the daimyos hired ninjas to carry out their plans.

Rise of the Ninja

From the mid-1400s through the early 1600s, Japan endured more civil war. This era was known as the

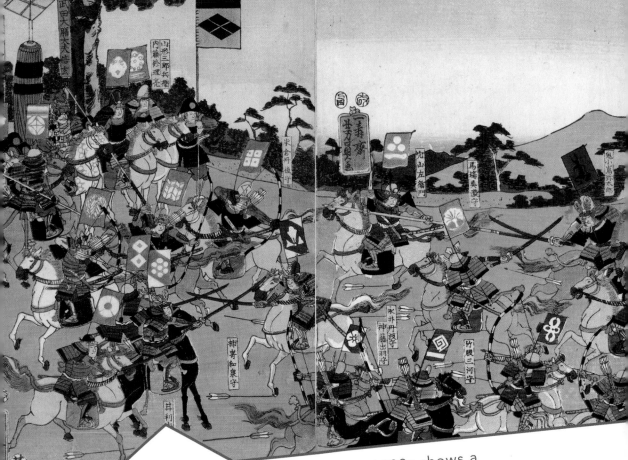

A piece of Japanese art from the 1800s shows a battle during the Sengoku Period, a time of great conflict across Japan.

Sengoku Period. Daimyos fought each other for land and power. Daimyos used ninjas as spies, scouts, surprise attackers, and assassins. Daimyos sent ninjas on missions to murder enemy daimyos. They launched night raids on enemy armies. They caused confusion in enemy ranks before an attack.

Ninjas could move quickly and quietly. They could disguise themselves to gain valuable information. They could fight with weapons and without weapons. Unlike the samurai, the ninjas were willing to do whatever it took to complete a mission. These hard-earned skills made the ninjas important to the daimyos who hired them.

FURTHER EVIDENCE

There is a lot of information about ninjas in Chapter Two. If you could pick out the main point of the chapter, what would it be? Find a few pieces of key evidence from the text that support the main point. Then explore the Web site below to learn even more about the history of ninjas. Find a quote from the Web site that supports the chapter's main point. Does this quote support an existing piece of evidence in the chapter? Or does it add a new piece of evidence? Why?

Ninja Kids

www.winjutsu.com/ninjakids/nk_history.html

CHAPTER THREE

BECOMING A NINJA

Ninjas came from a variety of backgrounds. Many ninjas were poor farmers who learned ninjutsu skills. Ninjas were paid well for their work. Other ninjas were former samurai who had abandoned their lords and the samurai code. Some ninjas came from families whose members had worked as ninjas for generations.

To become a ninja, one had to learn the art of ninjutsu.

Each family or group of ninjas developed its own traditions. These traditions and knowledge were called a *ryu*, or school of ninjutsu. Each ryu had its own rules and special techniques.

Iga and Koga Ninjas

Some of the most famous ryus emerged in central Japan. This area was known as the Iga and Koga provinces. The land was full of wooded valleys protected by steep mountains. The Iga-ryu and Koga-ryu became famous as training grounds for professional ninjas. In Iga and Koga, the ninjas lived in clans or families.

Ninja Skills

Ninjas needed to have great physical skills. A ninja had to be able to run long distances. He needed to swim across rivers and moats. He had to be ready to climb tall trees and walls. A ninja also needed to move quickly and quietly.

No matter what the situation was, a ninja moved with complete control. To gain control over his movement, a ninja learned different ways to walk. Each style could be

Tourists can visit the ninja museum in Japan's Iga province to see what daily life was like for an Iga ninja.

used in a different situation. Some ninjas practiced walking on a floor covered with paper until they walked without making any noise.

Ninjas hoped they would never need to fight. Most avoided open combat at all costs. A ninja tried to perform his mission without being seen or heard. To do this, a ninja was sometimes forced to lie in the same position for hours, or even days. All the while, he kept in complete silence so no one would suspect he was there.

Ninjas learned to control their breathing so they would not be heard. They practiced hiding behind rocks, in reeds, on roofs, in trees, and even under water. Ninjas used shade and stillness to blend into their surroundings.

Flying Ninjas

Many myths claimed ninjas could fly. Actually ninjas could just jump very well. Good jumping skills helped a ninja get over very high walls very quickly. A ninja practiced jumping over a wall using a partner's hands as a launching pad. He also trained with several ninjas to form a human pyramid. Ninjas used the pyramid to run up and over the wall. Ninjas also practiced using spears, pikes, or poles to vault over high walls.

Iranian women practice ninjutsu skills. Ninjas used these skills to appear as if they were flying.

Survival Skills

Ninjas often worked alone or in small groups. During an operation, a ninja could spend days alone hiding or traveling in the wilderness. One ninja trick was cooking rice without a pot. A ninja soaked the rice, wrapped it in leaves, and then buried it underneath a campfire. A ninja purified seawater by boiling it in an unglazed earthenware pot. The pot soaked the salt out of the water.

Ninjas were clever in their homes. This model of a ninja's house has many spots where ninjas could hide their weapons and tools.

Ninjas studied which plants and berries were edible and which could be used as poisons. Ninjas could use tree rings or stars as navigation tools. They counted their strides to calculate how far they had traveled. A ninja could tell time by using the position of the sun and an object's shadow.

Acting and Disguise

A ninja also learned the art of disguise. Disguises allowed him to travel without being recognized. A ninja chose the disguise that best fit his surroundings. He might dress as a beggar, farmer, soldier, or fisherman. Other common disguises included traveling merchants, musicians, priests, and entertainers.

Once in costume, a ninja learned to act the part. He had to be convincing in his role. A ninja learned the skills he would need to portray that role. For example, a ninja learned to sing and play an instrument well when disguised as a musician. He memorized prayers and religious ceremonies to dress as a priest.

When ninjas were on missions, they dressed the part. A ninja's outfit was simple. Everything was designed for a ninja to move easily without being noticed. For night missions, black, dark blue, or green clothing allowed ninjas to blend into the shadows.

Traditional Ninja Costume

A ninja's costume was a simple but useful outfit. Take a look at the ninja above. How might the design of his outfit help him during a mission? How would the outfit's design help him perform the skills talked about in this chapter?

A ninja wore a hood wrapped around his head so that only the face around the eyes could be seen.

Ninjas were trained to be stealthy. They were also trained to be dangerous. A ninja might prefer hiding and stealth to fighting. But all ninjas were prepared for battle if the situation called for it.

Ninja Natori Masazumi wrote *Shoninki*, a ninja training manual, in 1681. In the passage below, Natori discusses the best techniques for spying, using water birds as an example:

> *Water birds and other wild animals are often seen around castles and their moats, stone walls, and other hard-to-reach places where spies will surely take up position. If a noise is heard, it is most often birds taking off in flight.*
>
> *During the times that spies conceal themselves around castles, the birds fly off, the sky becomes cloudy, and the light of the stars wanes. Spying means blending in with the widest variety of things and, in this way, concealing yourself skillfully and with art.*
>
> Source: Natori Masazumi. Shoninki: The Secret Teachings of the Ninja. *Trans. Jon E. Graham. Rochester, VT: Destiny, 2009. Print. 72.*

What's the Big Idea?

Take a close look at Natori's words. What is his main idea? What evidence does Natori use to support his point? Come up with a few sentences showing how Natori uses evidence to support his main point.

CHAPTER FOUR

NINJA ATTACK

Ninjas were trained in martial arts. They learned how to use a variety of tools and weapons. A ninja also learned how to fight and defend himself without weapons. A ninja's style of fighting was meant to be flexible. A ninja could adapt to his opponent's fighting style. Then he used his opponent's weaknesses against him.

A modern ninjutsu master teaches ninja fighting techniques at a school near Tokyo, Japan.

Ninja Signals

Ninjas used signals to send messages back to their headquarters. Sometimes, they scattered colored rice on the ground. The combination of colors meant simple messages such as "all clear." Other times, ninjas played special coded songs to pass on a message.

Ninja Tools

A ninja often needed special tools on missions. Ladders and hooked ropes helped a ninja scale walls. Hand claws made it easier to climb wooden surfaces or trees. Spikes for the feet also gripped surfaces as the ninja scaled walls. A variety of flotation devices helped a ninja cross the water.

Ninjas eavesdropped on the enemy with a device similar to an ear trumpet. A ninja could hear valuable information by listening in. He could also listen to guards' movements.

Weapons

A ninja moved quickly and quietly. This meant his weapons had to be easy to carry and hide. Many weapons had multiple uses.

A katana sword's scabbard, or holder, could be used to hold tools or even as an underwater snorkel.

One of a ninja's most important weapons was his katana sword. The katana was a medium-length sword, usually about 20 inches (51 cm) long. The ninja drew a katana to strike the enemy or defend himself.

Tekagi were metal devices ninjas wore on their fingers. Tekagi often had claws, spines, or hooks attached. The ninja could hide his tekagi easily. Then he could surprise and strike his opponent.

A sickle and chain were made from a length of chain. A blade was attached to one end of the chain and a weight to the other end. The chain and weight could knock an opponent off of his feet. The ninja then stabbed him with the blade.

If a shuriken's tips were dipped in poison, it could even kill an attacker.

The *shuriken* was one of the best-known ninja weapons. The shuriken was a star-shaped throwing knife. It was small enough that a ninja could hide it in his hand. He could throw the shuriken to distract or delay the enemy while he escaped.

Ninjas also used fire and explosives as weapons. Fire spread panic and confusion. Ninjas shot fire arrows and threw fire sticks. A ninja could also fill a short piece of bamboo with gunpowder to make an explosive. A ninja used smoke bombs to create diversions and escape.

With these tools, skills, and deadly weapons, a ninja was ready to complete any mission for which his daimyo paid him.

EXPLORE ONLINE

Chapter Four discussed ninja weapons. The Web site for the Iga-Ryu Ninja Museum explores a similar topic. What information does the Web site give about a ninja's weapons? How is the information from the Web site the same as the information in Chapter Four? What new information did you learn from the Web site?

Ninja Iga
www.iganinja.jp/en

CHAPTER FIVE

NINJA MISSIONS

Japanese daimyos hired ninjas to perform many missions. A ninja's mission was usually a short-term operation. He had a specific goal or action to perform. He might sneak inside a castle. Then he could set a fire or learn about the castle's defenses. He might scout the enemy army. Or he might assassinate a rival.

A man makes a ninja sign with his fingers. Ninjas sometimes used secret signals to focus their mental and spiritual energies.

A Dangerous Assassin

One of the most famous stories about a ninja assassination is the mysterious death of Uesugi Kenshin. According to ninja records, Uesugi was a powerful daimyo. He had many enemies. He kept his guard close at all times. One night Uesugi entered his bathroom alone. According to legend, a ninja sent by a rival daimyo waited hidden in the sewer beneath the toilet. When Uesugi sat on the toilet, the ninja stabbed his backside with a sword. Uesugi howled in pain and collapsed. The mysterious assassin escaped unseen.

Castle Infiltration

Daimyos often hired ninjas to infiltrate and storm the castles of rival daimyos. Ninjas could cross moats, climb castle walls, and cut through doors and walls. They could creep across the castle grounds without being seen.

Once inside a castle, the ninjas could learn about the castle defenses and layout. They could cause chaos by setting fires, stealing items, or murdering important officials. They could also take out castle defenses before a daimyo's main army attacked.

Spies and Sabotage

Japanese daimyos knew espionage could give them an advantage during a war. Unlike a samurai, a ninja was willing to hide in the shadows and spy. Spying became one of the ninjas' most important missions. A ninja used his disguise skills to hide in crowds. He tricked his way into enemy castles and homes. Then he gathered valuable information about the enemy and its defenses.

The Art of Disguise

In 1558 daimyo Rokkaku Yoshikata hired a group of ninja warriors to infiltrate and attack a rival daimyo's castle. There were too many guards protecting the castle for a direct attack. Instead the ninjas snuck into the castle. They stole a lantern with the castle family crest. The ninjas made several copies of the lantern. Then they disguised themselves as guards. Carrying the fake lanterns, they calmly walked past the guards and into the castle. Once inside the ninjas set fire to the castle.

Ninjas also set out on missions to sabotage an enemy's camp, castle, or home. Ninjas often used fire to sabotage the enemy. The inside of a castle was often made with wood, straw, or paper. These materials burned easily and caused chaos.

During the Sengoku Period, powerful daimyos hired bodyguards to protect them day and night. To get past the bodyguards in order to get rid of powerful rivals, many daimyos turned to ninja assassins. The deadly assassins used speed and stealth to strike when least expected.

Decline of the Ninja

In 1603 Tokugawa Ieyasu became Japan's new shogun. Tokugawa was a strong leader. Wars between the daimyos ended. Peace soon spread throughout Japan. Ninjas occasionally still acted as spies for the shogun. But they were no longer in high demand.

Many ninjas turned to farming and other trades. By the 1800s, ninjas mostly existed in Japanese stories and folklore. The final recorded ninja mission

Tokugawa Ieyasu brought Japan into an era of peace. Daimyos no longer needed ninjas to storm castles or assassinate rivals.

took place in 1853. A US naval ship, commanded by Commodore Matthew Perry, arrived off the coast of Japan. Ninja Yasusuke Sawamura snuck onto the ship to try to learn why the commodore had come to Japan.

The great ninja warrior may have faded away. But the legend of the ninja lives on. The art of ninjutsu

Ninja warriors are no longer used in military operations. But people still study the art of ninjutsu at martial arts schools around the world.

is still portrayed in writings and scrolls. Ninjas are an important part of popular culture around the world. They have been the subject of comic books, movies, television shows, art, and more.

Although true ninja warriors no longer exist, people attend training camps to learn self-defense techniques based on ninjutsu. Some modern-day warriors, including US Navy SEALs, use elements of ninjutsu when they launch surprise attacks. While ninjas may have faded away centuries ago, the world's fascination with them is as strong as ever.

Ninjas were expert spies. Natori Masazumi's *Shoninki* covered the technique of faking an illness to gain access to an enemy's home:

The illnesses that you can use to your advantage this way are the stomach aches caused by worms, sunstroke, gastric distress, a heart attack, or diarrhea. It is not advisable to pretend to be drunk. After having obtained boiling water and pretending that you feel better, you should seize this opportunity to be taken inside the house and make the acquaintance of the master of the household while presenting a respectful attitude, and then leave the house.

You should next return with a gift, expressing the deepest of gratitude, and give the master of the house a letter of thanks. Once this is done, you can draw closer.

Source: Natori Masazumi. Shoninki: The Secret Teachings of the Ninja. Trans. Jon E. Graham. Rochester, VT: Destiny, 2009. Print. 57–58.

Consider Your Audience

Read the passage above closely. How could you adapt Natori's words for a modern audience, such as your neighbors or your classmates? Write a blog post giving this same information to the new audience. What is the most effective way to get your point across to this audience? How is the language you use for the new audience different from Natori's original text? Why?

IMPORTANT DATES AND BATTLES

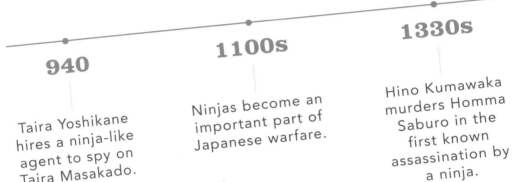

940

Taira Yoshikane hires a ninja-like agent to spy on Taira Masakado.

1100s

Ninjas become an important part of Japanese warfare.

1330s

Hino Kumawaka murders Homma Saburo in the first known assassination by a ninja.

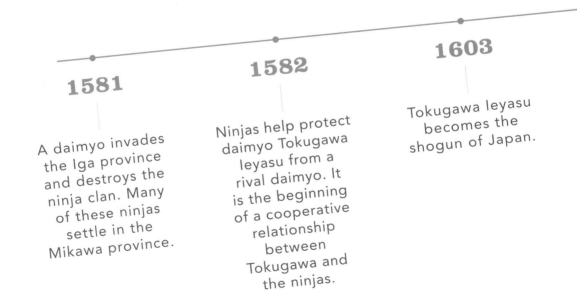

1581

A daimyo invades the Iga province and destroys the ninja clan. Many of these ninjas settle in the Mikawa province.

1582

Ninjas help protect daimyo Tokugawa Ieyasu from a rival daimyo. It is the beginning of a cooperative relationship between Tokugawa and the ninjas.

1603

Tokugawa Ieyasu becomes the shogun of Japan.

Mid-1400s

A time of chaos called the Sengoku Period begins.

1558

Rokkaku Yoshikata's hired ninjas sneak into and burn a rival daimyo's castle.

1562

Ninjas raid Tokugawa Ieyasu's rival's castle and take hostages.

1681

Ninja Natori Masazumi writes the *Shoninki*, a ninja training manual.

1800s

Ninjas are rarely used in warfare. They become part of Japanese folklore.

1853

Ninja Yasusuke Sawamura boards a US naval ship.

Why Do I Care?

Ninjas may have lived a long time ago. But a ninja's life might not be so different from yours. Have you ever worked hard to learn a new skill? Think about two or three ways the life and activities of a ninja connect to your own life. Write down a few examples of parts of your life that have a connection to ninjas.

Dig Deeper

What questions do you still have about ninjas? Do you want to learn more about their weapons? Or their training? Write down one or two questions to guide you in doing research. With an adult's help, find a few reliable new sources about ninjas that can help answer your questions. Write a few sentences about how you did your research and what you learned from it.

Another View

There are many sources about ninjas. Ask a librarian or another adult to help you find another source about ninjas and ninjutsu. Write a short essay comparing and contrasting the new source's point of view with this book. What is the point of view of each author? How are they similar? How are they different? Why might they be different?

You Are There

Imagine you are a young ninja living in Japan in the 1500s. Write 300 words describing your life. What do you see happening in your town? What are your siblings doing? What is a day in your life like?

GLOSSARY

assassin
someone who kills a person
of importance

daimyo
land-owning Japanese lord

deceit
dishonesty

discipline
commitment to strict training
for moral character and
mental and physical ability

elite
the best of a group

espionage
the act of spying

infiltrate
sneak or force into enemy
territory

mercenaries
soldiers paid to fight

ninjutsu
the set of fighting skills used
by ninjas

sabotage
disable or disrupt something

samurai
an upper-class Japanese
warrior

shogun
the general of the emperor's
army

stealth
a sly or secret action

LEARN MORE

Books

Levy, Joel. *Ninja: The Shadow Warrior.* New York: Sterling, 2008.

Olhoff, Jim. *Ninja.* Edina, MN: ABDO, 2008.

Turnbull, Stephen R., and James Field. *Real Ninja: Over 20 True Stories of Japan's Secret Assassins.* New York: Enchanted Lion, 2008.

Web Links

To learn more about ninjas, visit ABDO Publishing Company online at **www.abdopublishing.com**. Web sites about ninjas are featured on our Book Links page. These links are routinely monitored and updated to provide the most current information available.

Visit **www.mycorelibrary.com** for free additional tools for teachers and students.

INDEX

ABOUT THE AUTHOR

Carla Mooney is the author of several books for young readers. She loves investigating and learning about little-known people, places, and events in history. A graduate of the University of Pennsylvania, she lives in Pittsburgh, Pennsylvania, with her husband and three children.